THE DENTING OF A WAVE

RALPH THOMPSON

THE DENTING OF A WAVE

PEEPAL TREE

First published in Great Britain in 1992
Peepal Tree Books
17 Kings's Avenue
Leeds LS6 1QS
Yorkshire
England

© Ralph Thompson 1992

All rights reserved
No part of this publication may be
reproduced or transmitted in any form
without permission

ISBN 0 948833 62 9

FOR

DODY AND THE CHILDREN

ACKNOWLEDGEMENTS

Some of these poems originally appeared in *The Gleaner, Carib 5, Jamaica Journal, Kyk-over-Al, The Caribbean Writer* and *The London Magazine*.

CONTENTS

Carpenters	9
Ablutions	11
Cycling	13
Fences	14
Harbour View	15
Rain	16
Hurricane	17
'He Knows What Height Is'	19
Death of a Honda Rider	21
Cavafy at Terra Nova	22
Walking at 4 a.m.	24
The Road	26
Jamaica Farewell	27
The Forest Is Your Life	28
Florida	29
Sanibel Beach	30
Refuge	31
The Crane	32
The Virgin Mary at Wellesley College	34
Icarus at Cape Canaveral	36
Leda	39
Sally	40
After Love	41
Waiting	42
Anniversary	43
After Dinner	44
Anatomy Lesson	46
On Turning Fifty	47
In Contemplation of a Poet's Head	48
Homo Sapiens Prime	49
For Mothers	50
For Sons	51
Questions	52
My God	53

Sufficiencies	54
Priorities	55
Morning Mass in a Kingston	56
On the Death of a Fish	58
Reflections	59
Time and Tide	62
Feeling Slightly Ill-at-Ease in Someone else's House	63
Clocks	65
What the Cloud Saw	66
Silence	67
Kingston/Baghdad	69
Ars Longa	73
Mr. Goodman's Last Visit Abroad	75
The Other Island	82

CARPENTERS

Years ago when I had nothing else to do
except to ogle back at tree ghosts in a forest
about a mile along the road from Hardwar Gap,
my friend, Malcolm, who had long inhabited
a shack that rotted in the ferns and bracken bush
undertook to build a one-room timber house
and to this end employed the services and skills
of Mr. Coombs, a carpenter from Silverhill.

I was ten, Malcolm incalculably old
and purple black. I was nearly white
but now I know we shared a rare astonishment —
he at the prospect of a house respectable
enough in which to die and me at Mr. Coombs
pegging out a new domain with such casual
grace and squint-eyed wisdom as Penn & Venables
would have envied, albeit this forest colony
was twelve by sixteen feet of mildewed mulch.

Pencil tucked behind his ear, Mr. Coombs
bends over a beam bridging two inverted
forty-gallon drums — its yellow fur erect, ready for
the razor tongue of plane to shave its splinters,
to peel its skin down to the smell of pine and pitch
while Mr. Coombs up to his unlaced boots in clay
whistles through gold-capped teeth, blessing with
flicks of sweat the curtilage of Malcolm's plot.

I stand, the dim light cupping my face back
as, hand over hand, columns are raised and braced.
Hammer strokes explode the silver heads of nails
and every time the carpenter's right arm shoots up
I blink, never knowing if the sparks I see —
red and blue — are real or only in my head.

Mr. Coombs plucks a chalked cord like a taut
harp string, aligning horizontals on the soil's
black skin. Swinging a piece of twine tied to a rock
he sights for honest perpendiculars.
While Mr. Coombs lays down the floor and Malcolm
cuts rubber strips from an abandoned tyre to hinge
the door (rubber like silence does not rust in woods)
I am allowed the apprenticeship of scraps.
With two lengths of surplus laths and rusty nails
I make the primal shape, only slightly
out of true but right enough for showing off.

In eight weeks Malcolm takes possession of his
home, celebrating title and completion
with Mr. Coombs and a bottle of white rum.
I am invited in, noticing the warmth
of timbered in-ness. Hardly listening to the drift
of their post mortem, I choose the toolbox as my stool
pondering the career of carpenters.

ABLUTIONS

A pipe jutted like a gibbet from
the outside kitchen wall above a shallow
cistern and when in the cool of early schoolboy
mornings its silver rope of water whipped
its chill around my throat, choking off
the involuntary scream, I wondered
why poverty ordained such ritual
ablutions and, anointing crotch with red
carbolic soap, cherished a hope the girl
next door would peek around the corner,
pretending indignation.

        I claimed this time and place
and all its dispensations by right of water
and since the world still slept I willed that she
should float across the fence and lift a foot
into the cistern. Through the curtain
of her hair I watched the water runnel
from her breasts, flowing into a new
and nervous valley, beading the matted
pubic hair with pearls. Then she was gone
and I, mouth salivaless and dry,
walked on heels across the dusty yard
back into the snoring house.

It seems so long ago, those days of cold ablutions,
their rapture stamped upon my memory
like the pattern of a fern on skin —
pain and pleasure wired in a silver
circuit of fusion and confusion,
passion and compassion and the rueful
knowledge that since my sudsing took a richer

turn I have scrubbed away the coin
of her face.

      Could what they say about
cold showers still be true if this poem
only tingles into life at the
remembered shock of early morning water.

CYCLING

Dressing for school —
open collared shirt, jock strap,
susurrus and sheen of short
khaki pants so fiercely
starched they stood up by themselves,
foot forced to tear a path
between the cloth to pull them on.

The leap upon the bike —
feeling the animation of its steel
between my legs, pedal elevated,
head hanging over handle bars
curved like the horns of Afghan sheep,
geared for the gravity of hills,
rocking from side to side.

Then the glide —
down South Camp Road
spokes spinning in refracted light,
such trust between the rider and the ridden
no hands were needed,
mere inclination was enough
to steer, mere wish sufficient
for the swish of wheels.

One night I rode my bike
right up Blue Mountain to the peak —
such an exhausting dream,
pumping, pumping, pumping.

FENCES
(Reflections on a Gun Court)

The house is sitting on its haunches
like an ancient market woman
taken short along the way,
suspicious windows squinting into
a harsh, unblinking morning sun.

It has a ten-foot dildo fence
and hedges of aralia
flanked less against a trespasser
than to keep the dogs inside
And me as well.

Back then the trams
clanged their chains up South Camp Road
shuddering the house. Its seams
were opening and in revenge
one night I aimed my water pistol
through the fence, arching a stream
into the pool of someone's lap.

That was fifty years ago
and now the house and tracks are gone.
But every morning on my way
to work I pass the site. I see
a red facade glinting the guns
of sterling chaps who guard the turrets
and the chain-link fences sprung
from decayed aralias.
A few dead dildos and if they found
my boyhood water pistol in the
car, I would be quite at home.

HARBOUR VIEW

Beyond the edge of my window
overlooking the harbour
the prow of a red cargo boat
floats without motion
on the blue water.

The steel hull is smooth
and looms immovable above
the agitated
surface of the sea surrounding it.

No one part, neither the longitude of the boat,
the nervous petulance of the water
nor the colour of each
is strong enough to break the tension
Of the picture's composition
locked into the frame of the window.

But it will not last.
Either the ship,
eaten up with demurrage,
will sink or sail
or the sea,
in conspiracy with the wind,
will push the red prow back
and thus prevail,
or I, unable to be a witness to defeat
will close the curtain.

RAIN

The rain this afternoon was loud.
Like grain scattered by a giant
fist it beat upon the roof,
too belligerent for sleep.

My wife winding windows up
suppressed the pecking of the drops
yet the wetting widened slowly
soaking like a stain into
the cedar shingles, uncurling them.

After an hour we sprung a leak.
It beaded pearls along the beam
then, like a broken rosary,
fell spattering the sheet.

I was not astounded. Water
is democratic and it found
its level beside me on the bed.

HURRICANE

Now I am the still centre of my
raging self, eye
of the hurricane that roared
from between my mother's thighs
whirling my name across the map
of its dominion, track-
ing the coordinates of conscience,
bending the will
like trees under a battering of wind.

The land was drenched and the sea
poured over the rocks of my years,
furious, unrelenting,
the white spume twisting up
then falling back like tears.
In green squalls
I wept for what I had demolished
yet dreamed of new destruction
in vast circulating waves of want.

I remember praying for exhaustion
when the mountains muscled their backs
against the forward fury,
stalemating 'yes' and 'no'.
But appalled at such a marriage of convenience
I blasted on.

Now the eye's still centre!
How long will this calm last?
No hurricane has time to ask
so desperate a question.
But the rocks have been eroded,
the days dimmed,
an asylum found.

In the eye, because it is rimmed
with vision, I can see the sun
and because it is wet with silence
I can hear the winds whispering my name —
waiting to roar again.

'HE KNOWS WHAT HEIGHT IS'
(FOR LOUIS SIMPSON)

He knows what height is, this hillside dweller
who squints occasionally at the waving sea
below, the lustre of its greener
eye engulfing the valley to return his gaze.
One day, hacking at high vines
he saw his cutlass hanging in the sky,
motionless, an off-course Air Jamaica
plane aimed at the airport. He has never
flown, assumes that those who do by looking down
can bless or cast a spell upon the ground.

High is the axed pine that pitches forward
shivering like a compass needle in the circle
of the clearing, pulled true north to where the bird,
a Solitaire, like him a mountain exile,
flutes its two-note elegy, centre
of lamentation in which his hut is huddled.
At dusk he slides down the slope from field
to shack, leaning back against the incline,
heels hugging dirt, a trickle of stones
rolling before him into the ravine.

He sits alone at sunset, the hills hunched
around him leaking purple, the black crack
of the gorge narrowing to a scar stitched
into the mountain's back. Clinging to the brink
of the precipice his hut is a wattled
blink of lantern light behind
the streaming banners of the evening mist.
Then suddenly the bird — a black silken
knot unravelling down the valley! Free,
it rocks on the scooped air. Then
as he knows it will, dips, followed by a

fury of ascent, arching up
contemptuous of gravity, swift
and pure as the crescent curve of his machete.
At another time, another edge, he watched
his mother climb a guinep tree, skirt
billowing in the breeze and from a limb
lower a swing for him, sisal knotted
under a wooden slat. Higher and higher
she pushed him into terrifying air.

The bird floats down the mountain, wings at rest,
riding high currents over the ridges, swinging
him between the peaks, feet dangling
above the abyss filling up with shadows,
elbows screaming at his sides,
fingers frozen on the fog frayed vines.
As it was in the beginning so, after all
these years, the sign and wonder — between his legs
the anus closing, the shrinking of the balls.

DEATH OF A HONDA RIDER

From a pothole's asphalt vase
a sprig of red hibiscus waves
the traffic off. A Honda rider,
knees splayed, grinning his route
through black self-generated air
floats his teeth across the windscreen
of the car in hot pursuit
of someone he desires or despises
more than us, the butt
of a revolver tucked into
his belt under the billowing shirt.

How soon before they stumble on his body
in a gully, the front wheel
of the Honda spinning slowly,
the engine ticking as it cools?

Air palpable as oil
from the cracked crank case
lubricates the black descending
of the crows. Whatever dreams
he dreams lying on his back
still exact the rictus smile
that lashed the corners of his mouth
to the centre of his skull
where, under Rasta locks, his truth
was hidden and a million
revelations, spliff certified,
flared to a faith you could not face
unless you dared to ride the pillion.

CAVAFY AT TERRA NOVA

Cavafy sat in his spats at Terra Nova
his white suit tailored
from a large table cloth
peeled of the pearl of its damask,
watching a tight-bottomed busboy
serving a couple of tourists.

Everyone else had abandoned their stations.
The captain who for years
buried his tips in a tin can
to avoid paying taxes
was digging furiously in the dark garden
to recapture his cache.

Cooks postponed soaking plum puddings
and although not a war cry was throated
farmers prepared for the scorching of crops
crouching like relay runners
waiting for rumours and matches.

Businessmen cremated their minute books
anxious to face new eras
with clean hands and ledgers.
A number of sage civil servants
blew out their brains with unsuspected flair
while priests high and low
consumed their wafers in fear
of the advancing host.

When the tight-assed busboy
serving soup with trembling hands,
asked Cavafy what was wrong,
were the barbarians coming after all,

Cavafy dabbed his lips and sighed
recalling that some time ago
he had composed a small piece
which might be apropos.
He had a copy in his valise
which, after dinner, if the boy
was really interested
he would be happy to explain.

Cavafy sat in his spats in a corner,
the busboy beside him like a question mark,
the room's remainder
a still life of tables
without spoons or plates
reserved for the late arrival of barbarians.

WALKING AT 4 A.M.

At the Pegasus hotel I walk
(too old for jogging) in the dark,
the track picked out with cannon balls
enamelled white, half buried, looping
like a strand of imitation pearls
around the pool, cornering
the sculpture of a whitewashed rock,
levelling through a row of palms
wainscotted white, bending beside
a backless concrete bench stretched
taut as a tomb under a lignum
vitae tree whose silhouette
is a skull spiked on a bark blotched neck.

A St. Elizabeth red woman
moon, arms folded across
her breast, full of bile, glares
like a jealous wife at the hotel
suspicious of infidelities.
Street lamps outside the chain-link fence
bloom like agapanthus lilies
and from this confluence of light
the shadows spring, my body breaking
at the ankles, testing the height
of hedges, sidling the trunks of tree,
scissoring the lawn with stilts. Cowled stalker,
mad monk at matins, I cloud a wave
across the pool, walking on water.

A cloud covers the moon's cracked grin
and yellow teeth. In the demi-dark
the shadow of a tall tree's limb
feathered with leaves, dihedral wing,

undulates against the slabbed high wall
of the hotel. How many mornings
have I shared its flight,
spectral bird in perpetual
migration? Suddenly
someone speaks my name, softly
but unmistakably. A shadow
cowled like me invades the track,
for a moment mingling lip to lip
with mine, then fades to a retreating back.

'200 meters to a Guinness' —
just reward for the lurching verses
of a poet panting to his heart's
alarming S.O.S.
The giant phantom wing flaps faster
seeking sanctuary. The freshening breeze
bullies a serviette hiding
from last night's poolside party,
swirls it like a kite until
it slams against the chain-link fence
where it hangs, back impaled
high upon the wire, a white
flag of surrender fluttering
in the kingdom of the shadows.

THE ROAD

A road guarded by a row
of trees, running through
their ranks, has run too long
and comes, panting, to a dead end,
to a peeling sign that reads
'Trespassers will be shot' —
no dialogue about abandoned
hope, just the skeleton
of an iron gate draped
with barbed wire, locked.

JAMAICA FAREWELL

What I remember
is the sun-crazed summer
that you said good-bye,
light filed to the fine
fury of a machete
slicing open the eye
of the sea, slashing at our faces
as we drove across the city.

'Why am I going,
Genes or geography?'
you asked, tracing an alien
map with your fingers
on my cheek. Even
without tears its borders
blurred and disappeared.

An indifferent Kingston
flushed itself into the harbour
silting up the ocean
with departures. The road
curled around the airport
like a question mark,
its meagre wrist of land
as fragile as your embracing hands.

'THE FOREST IS YOUR LIFE'

In the timbered light
of this secluded wood,
burdened with poems too obese
for such an impoverished land,
I am running to edit myself,
toeing the line of a red pencilled path
in terror of its cancellation.

On the hill behind the military
barracks, platoons of pines
dress ranks for the inspection
of the axe. Tomorrow they will sprawl
upon the slopes, their corpses
locked in that embrace which shawls
the fallen from Jamestown
to Tegucigalpa. Among the dead,
ginger lilies gleam like red
menorah exhaling the sickly
sweet perfume of death.

Outside the hydro station
a guard hunkers barefoot
on the gravel, an M16
across his lap, a Panasonic
wailing Spanish songs
into his ear. Above his head,
nailed to a tree, a Ministry
of Propaganda sign proclaims
'el bosque es tu vida'
and already in a land accustomed
to command the saplings spring.
In Honduras, ginger lilies smell of pine.

FLORIDA

I am walking in a subdivision
dubbed 'the elms' in which there are no trees
and the houses line the street in fenceless
duplication, so anxious to avoid
the sweat of living all their dust and draft
are packed in garbage pans equipped with wheels.

Outside the kitchen walls air-conditioners
crouch like frogs on concrete pads croaking
in the morning heat. At one corner
a red-bowlered fire hydrant impersonates
Toulouse-Lautrec guarding the abandoned
condom of a newspaper wrapped
in cellophane. At the other, a flaccid
American flag, pro bono publico,
is shafted by a thin aluminium pole.

The doors of the garages lift open on
command, saying 'aah' for the inspection
of tools aligned like teeth along the walls.
Yesterday the kids were playing hopscotch
on the sidewalk and in one square
a red tricycle gleams like a
triumphant taw. It could have been
a red wheel barrow but this is not the Paterson
geography. Only the black barrels
engorged with garbage roll.

SANIBEL BEACH

I, who am a watcher of horizons
from way back or at least as far
as the tether of my pride prescribes,
stand on the shore at Sanibel
watching the sea arch the bow
of this horizon, hearing the stereophonic
waves pour into the ears of shells.
They shake the water out and I
am conscious of encirclement.
Over the gulf a chord of sky
tightens the ocean, tuning the waves
to a higher pitch. Like all prisoners
I am the staked epicentre of a cell
looking out at a bent world —
waiting for parole.

REFUGE

To find yourself a stranger
in the blurred geography
of a half-remembered city
and, taken short,
in a moment of panic
to single out an office tower
and deflecting down an unmarked corridor
to push a private door
opening upon a hermitage
of gleaming cubicles
into one of which you lurch,
there in Lysoled, air-conditioned silence,
your shoes reflecting in the polished tile,
to take relief — as once an ancestor
fearing assault in such a vulnerable pose
scampered off the track
and squatting in high grass
the wind behind his back,
manured the forest, the filtered light
speckling his leaf encircled toes.

THE CRANE
(on being driven to hospital for surgery)

From the city's concrete edge
a solitary crane, naked,
angles X rated struts into the air
as if to fly, skeleton of wing
waiting only for the lift of skin.

A plane, glinting like a scalpel,
slices through the clouds
opening the eye
of an incision in the cheek
of this December sky.

It tears along the edges
of the crane whose metal thongs
rove a lanyard through
the lesion, lacing in
the maggotry of heaven.

If one thread snapped what
would fall from that dividing
sky? Croesus crouches
over the crack, shitting
golden guineas on Manhattan

till the second coming of Bosch.
'Bless me Father for I have sinned.
It has been at least six centuries
since my last confession'. Are these
the same gold coins that weighted
Hector's lids after his last ride?
How bravely all the ancients died
or had the race not yet invented
pain? While the crane

holds strain I should run
and dip my body in the healing
Hudson but this highway
will not let me off its stretcher.
The river fog rolls in
thick as anaesthetic.

It starts to rain. The wet sky
contracts, tightening the wound.
My eyes begin to close.
The great boom swings.
Oh, the stitchery of steel.

THE VIRGIN MARY AT WELLESLEY COLLEGE

Our daughter back home after a year
in Paris where we had visited with her
to celebrate her twenty-first,
had met her beau,
all four holding hands and dancing
down the hill from Sacre Coeur,
the April rain glazing
her blond hair, reminds us now
in a quiet interlude after coffee and cognac,
her laugh like a demure arpeggio,
of the time when she was eight years old
and the Virgin Mary appeared to her
sitting on the formica top
of the built-in dressing table —
not your classic face but a sweet smile,
tres triste, and the hushed imperative
about the curve her destiny would take.

The laugh again sliding up the scale
and the confession that in her Freshman
year at Wellesley, suddenly stricken
with pneumonia, alone in the infirmary
fighting not to drown in her own lungs,
she prayed to Mary
and when she woke up in the morning
the odour of disinfectants
had evaporated and the perfume of roses
blossomed in the ward
filling it with new sweet air
which she was able to inhale
but which the nurse,
possibly because her sinuses were blocked,
could not detect.

There was this long, half awkward silence
as under the magnification of beginning tears
her hazel eyes grew larger;
then the laugh again
and I thought that she —
undeniably touched —
should be writing this poem.

ICARUS AT CAPE CANAVERAL

Banished by Minos to a Cretan
concentration camp, there
were just the two of us, my dad
and me, to hoard the feathers and
to mould the wax. It was he
who first conceived that man can fly
and in that state of hubris fretted
for the lift of air. But bees
cannot be bullied into waxing
and Daedelus, allergic to
chickens, worked in fits. The feathers
rippled when he sneezed, their quills
impatient to record our flight.

At last we strapped the vellicating
wings upon our backs and like
two fledgling angels lifted up,
flapping above the upturned O
of an astonished farmer's mouth,
over a horse rubbing his rump
against a eucalyptus tree.
We tracked our bearings in the mirror
of a lake and banking east
beat toward the red corolla
of the sun.

          Freed at last
from earth and earth's iniquities,
vectored on the updraft of
impending myth, my spirit should
have soared for purer air. Instead,
the corners of my recollection
enclosed a rumpled bed guarded
by the statue of a wooden

cow, oozing at the nostrils,
its udders full as funeral urns.
Sculpted for her by Daedelus,
I had dared to cross its jealous
gaze. 'You are too young' he cried
carving me naked with his stare.
'You are too old' I might have shouted back
but age stuck in my throat like vomit.
Unperturbed, she gravely
pulled the linens to her chin.

I am the patron saint of falling
whose destiny was blinded
by the approaching sun. Even
from this great height of time and space
I did not see your satellite
descending to its death because
some white-smocked engineer, pining
for his Parsiphae, forgot
to tighten the essential bolt.

But do not pray to me for I
am fiction. Pray rather
that when your rockets fall
there will be souvenirs more solemn
than the denting of a wave.
In an age that forfeits myth
for science, souvenirs are treasured
more than icons. Without a piece
of metal on the shelf to fondle
you are condemned like me to poems.

Into the sun I flew, high
above my father, across whose back

my shadow rippled. At noon I felt
a dampness in my crotch like urine
but as the wetness seeped between
my legs I sniffed the fumes of melting
paraffin. Ancient custom
notwithstanding, I fell feet first,
feathers flickering around
my face like fireflies, ears
stuffed with wax, nostrils corked
with viscid air. All sight turned inward,
my eyes were blown back
into their sockets. Thus, as I
descended to the ocean I did not
hear the breaking waves,
nor taste their salt, nor see
their emerald fires flare to singe
my flesh.

        O Parsiphae, is it
with thee all flights begin and end.

LEDA

Why are we,
black daughters of Jamaica,
so afraid of lizards?
Confronted by such a wall
of prejudice I think
that they, the bloodless ones,
have climbed it with aplomb.

I have seen
some fall, of course, but only
rarely and even then
they rise with grace to the occasion,
sticking out their tongues
in half-amused contempt.

The angled head,
the hooded, ackee eyes,
ancestral lineaments
inherited from one
who scaled a garden wall
and gazing at a naked lady
felt the world's first blush
blistering his skin.

White girls deserve unruffled
long-necked swans.
Under a poinciana tree
I keep a crimson assignation.
With a parting of the leaves he comes
and in the red shade
this other Eve, breasts tightening,
is only half afraid.

SALLY

Flesh is a cheat.
Unzip it down the spine
To be discarded like a hostess gown,
Changed from brown to black to white
To match a man, a place, a time.
Why weep in a prison skin of lies?
Rise Sally rise and wipe your eyes.

Cushioned crab grass,
Green fingers tickling your back,
Cracked floorboards of a rolling sloop,
Pretty perfumed percale sheets —
What choice of bed
For love remembered, love realised?
Rise Sally naked. Sally rise.

AFTER LOVE

Spent in passion on the floor
I lie like a demolished church
about your feet, watching your eyes
trace in tenderness the rubble
of my body as if your carnal
knowledge of it is not enough.
Like an archaeologist
you must find its grand design,
its columns and its feet of clay;
the puzzle of a deeper lust
curls the corners of your mouth.
Since nothing less can satisfy
and nothing more is possible
I watch you close the notebook of your search.

WAITING

The bedside lamp splashes
your side of the room with light,
tracing the mould of your body
in the vacant bed,
filling the pillow's depression
and the pores of the chenille spread
with the scent of your elbows.

Your glasses, slightly out of shape,
pretend to read the open book
on which they rest,
making an empty spectacle of themselves
in the absence of your eyes.

On the bedside table
the telephone, silent and tense,
holds a hand over its mouth.

Goodnight when you come home!

I have missed you
as if you were away
for a long time
during which I grew interminably old
waiting for your return —
afraid to shut off the light.

ANNIVERSARY
(For Dody)

Do you remember all the cheering
when this tournament began?
The toasts, the songs? But we endured
too long. Even our seconds,
growing bored with such fidelity,
depart the lists while we joust on.

Toe to toe we have withstood
the years, embracing to the death.
Who cried first was traitor
till the armour of our laughter
rusted and each thrust thrust deeper
till we could thrust no more.

Locked too long in combat,
too weak to strike another blow
now do we truly fall in love.
Sprawled upon the greensward of our years
let us unbuckle and strew
our garments on this field.
Our gauntlets, thrown down, will spin
new skins for snakes,
Our helmets will be hives for bees.

AFTER DINNER
('Ripeness is all') *Lear*, V, II, ii

Two women after dinner, sewing,
exchanging embroidered conversation,
laughter like French knots edging the pattern
of an evening stretched between
benevolence and boredom.

A man, husband and father, mantled
in meditation, sits in silence
fingering the fabric of
his possibilities, centred
somewhere between memory
and imagination.

Suddenly, his passion needled
by a faulty thread of logic
in the lady's talk, he lurches
from his chair and like a mad
conductor beats the air

with the baton of his index finger.
Wife and daughter bent above
their sewing like two violinists
freeze on the upward bowing
of a stitch.

The thunder of his shouting shudders
the ceiling opening a crack
from which a filament of plaster
pearls a crown around his head,
the royal roar soaring beyond
the bounds of sympathy as if
his gestures really ruled the world.
'Darling, the neighbours...' 'FUCK

the neighbours, it is the principle
that counts.'

Exhaustion slips a noose around
his throat, choking the tempest from
his rage. He is a poet,
not a despot and certain births
are irreversible —

like beating back a butterfly
to chrysalis. He crumples on
the couch, the TV's iridescence
washing his cheeks in flashes
of diluted red.

The women's needles, re-opening
their eyes, reach up once more toward
the comfort of the cloth. Outside
a dog barks, a distant siren wails.

ANATOMY LESSON

Regard that woman's countenance, cold
as a mask. This is its genesis.
A sheet of skin peeled from a new roll
is pulled over the unfinished skull
tighter than a rubber glove around
the knuckles of a surgeon. Below the brow
a scalpel balanced to the horizontal
slices openings for eyes, the edges
bound like button holes with cat gut lashes.

Then the swift, unhesitating slash
for mouth, beads of blood bubbling like words
along the line of lip. Pain guides
the saga of incision and the tolling
of inner tongues as the blade, turning
to the vertical, lowers slowly
to the pelvic V. But that's another story.

ON TURNING FIFTY
(for John Hearne)

Midway (approximately) on the journey of your life,
take comfort that in stockinged feet
you, at the still anniversary of your birth,
can feel the world turning on its axis,
earth creeping over its own crescent
for the fiftieth time.

And as it starts its next descent
you, despite the weight of one more year,
another twelve month growth of things and sentiments,
will hardly speed its course.
So much for wisdom, age and grace!

That is the blessing of half-centuries —
wine left to breathe before the drinking,
love less frantic for the savouring,
friends more loyal for the keeping
and the greeting of anniversaries in wool socks
with much wriggling of toes in the turf of the earth
as it climbs once more up the other side.

IN CONTEMPLATION OF A POET'S HEAD
(On hearing that Derek Walcott has given up poetry for painting)

Those lands whose limits you have metered
to the beat of humming bird and eagle
line their geographies across your cheeks.
The skull, engineered for laurel leaves,
stressed now by new discoveries,
brow bulging, holds strain against a brain
in restless co-existence with idea and image.
If brow break so too the heart,
rapture like molten gold oozing through the crack
into the green eyes, down the flaring
ramparts of the nose, beading like tears
on the thick ledge of lip.
Rapture is a risk all poets take.
You alone with pen or pallet will compose
the balance of your days.
For the bronze armoury of bone give praise.

HOMO SAPIENS PRIME

On a cold Sunday
pew after pew of Grant Wood faces
peer through rimless spectacles
at a preacher
to whom they have surrendered
all their pitchforks
until Monday.

It will happen on such a clear
uncomplicated winter day —
trees, limbs lifted high,
frozen like giant pitchforks
unambiguously black
against the sky;
bowed backs at last
congealed to congregation,
a race raised to the prime —
still men enough for earth
but, perhaps, no longer man.

FOR MOTHERS

It may have been an immaculate conception
but the delivery was like any other —
blood-soaked, uncouth,
the knees spread,
the head flung back,
a strand of black hair
caught between the teeth.

Someone cut the cord
but that was not the end of it —
the last moan
floated up,
an O coated in cold air
filtering through the thatched roof.

How often have you warmed
that frozen note to life inside your womb,
the same pain
sweating your hair,
lips voweling that ancient sound
into new ears.

Your daughters have heard it,
while I
tone deaf and terrified
wait in the corridor
clutching flowers.

FOR SONS

The wild ride up
out of the womb
swinging, heels held,
to the pendulum chant
'It's a boy! It's a boy!'

The stirrup glints,
swinging like a censer
against the sweated flank.
From ancient dust
such a high mount!

The sun springs from the sea
glazing in bright witness
the blade that taps the shoulder.
'You have earned your spurs.
Arise, Sir Knight.'

The world grows strong,
rising from its knees
like a colt. Cowboys and kings,
all sons ascending
in whom we are well pleased.

QUESTIONS

The record is clear. He commanded
Lazarus to rise and so he did
but what of the four day interval?

Were there complications when the soul,
fatigued by its departure,
dazzled by divinity,
suddenly grasping the new glory,

was requested to return?
Did Lazarus at first refuse,
obliging God to emphasise
how foolish his friend

would look if the miracle backfired?
Did Lazarus like a reluctant child
mumble 'oh all right' and petulantly
picking up the winding sheet
drag his heels back to the grave?

And the next day —
examining his face before a mirror
was there a trace of worm tracks
to remind him of his unlikely journey?

MY GOD

The divine mind
contemplates the infinite will,
defines it in finite form
and time and space
become caesuras in the long line that poems forth,
the nib of the poised pen
still wet with words. Time
is space unravelling and space
is the time it takes to trace the limits
which the pen has shaped.

To be infinite is to contain
all contradiction —
love and indignation,
power and submission,
life and death.
But not repose.
God at the switch!
If he should doze
the energy of containment would explode,
blow up creation,
time and space echoing back to silence.
Homer nods
but not my God scripting His metaphors,
the poised pen descending.

SUFFICIENCIES

I think only as deep as puzzlement,
I feel but only to the edge of pain.

My fear extends
no further than where the unexpected shadow
bends the corner.

My tears are equal to my grief.
My ears no sharper than a sampled sound.

My legs are long enough, but only just,
to touch the ground.

PRIORITIES

Picture Da Vinci taking a photograph
of the Last Supper and as he ducks his head
under the black cloth behind the camera
the apostles in appreciation of the meal
hold their clean plates behind their heads.
This is the fantasy of a Parisian poet
and it has the ring of truth — not so much
about Da Vinci but of the French
who always put eating first.

MORNING MASS IN KINGSTON

The congregation sways
to a jazzed-up version of the great Amen,
clapping hands.
Then exultation ends.
All is hushed
except for the distant crowing of a cock
and the wheeze of oscillating fans
between the stations of the cross
dispensing breeze like holy water.

A girl with pink bows plaited in her hair,
combed into squares,
genuflects on thin black legs in ankle socks,
clutching a transparent plastic purse.

Outside, an old soldier of an ackee tree,
medalled with fruit,
flashes an emerald salute.
A Royal Palm points the imperial finger
of its shadow across the lawn.
A lizard thrashes through the grass
and dragon flies lift up on wings
the colour of clear glass.

The morning sun
bounces off the bumper of a green Toyota
parked underneath a mango tree
and blinds a nun shuffling music sheets.
She puts dark glasses on.
The Church, open on three sides,
is stoned with light.

The priest raises a black hand in blessing
and a blue nimbus
instantly ignites the curve of bowed black heads.
Pale fire
smoulders like a fuse down knuckled pews,
flickering from intoning lips:
'I have loved, O Lord, the beauty of your house
and the place where your glory dwells.'

The lifted host,
a ghostly azure disk,
glows at the edges.
The flock, except for me,
is candled in blue light.

The parish mongrel
ambles down the aisle
and seeking the refrigeration of cool tiles
stretches on his belly before the altar.
Do blue flames like hackles
ride his back?
I am afraid to look.

ON THE DEATH OF A FISH

A fish twists on a taut line
dripping its dying shadow on the sand,
the same beach on which millennia ago
a progenitor wriggled from the sea,
evolved,
and learned to bait a hook.

What sticks in the gullet
is not death
but time catching up with itself
to the applause of laughter
which rankles now inside the gills
like dirty water.

Except for the ridiculous gesture
of a jerking tail
all protest is denied,
imprisoned behind the misting
plate-glass eyes;
no tongue to spit defiance,
no voice to wail in lamentation,
no hands, even in surrender,
to sign the benediction of its ancient cross
into the alien air already thickening to wood.

REFLECTIONS
(for a Scottish Granddaughter)

I

In a basin under a window overlooking the orange
blessings of a rowan tree your mother rinsed
your hair and whispered that the colour from your curls

could turn the suds to gold. Sapphires and pearls,
she promised, would gem from blue-eyed tears, yours
to keep when crying ceased, to ornament

the bezel of those dreams she shares with you, dreamt
deep in the genes, still sleeping in my blood.
Such fragile fantasies stumble from the words

that make them up into the embrace of sounds
seeking their echoes, poetry before the poem,
ominous infection of the middle ear.

II

'She is enrolled in ballet school. This year
the Peebles beginners give their first recital'
your mother writes. 'She is elated!' Did you dream

of your début, pulled to that point between
performance and applause where every artist dies
until the first sharp clap, the laying on of hands

that signals resurrection? The neck unbends —
then that triumphant stiff-legged ballerina
march towards the footlights as toe blocks slap

the stage; a blown kiss, the tilted back
descending in a curtsy, eyes on the royal box,
arms folding across the heaving heart.

A later letter: 'Not an auspicious start
to her career, I am afraid. Tu-tued
and tighted, as the curtain lifted they lost

their nerve — there in the wings, legs crossed,
the Peebles corps de ballet sucking their thumbs
and pulling down their knickers. No tears, thank God.'

III

At Jedburgh when you were five years old, we trod
the Norman stones, the ruin battered to its knees
by bloody Border wars, half an ancient

wall still lifting a bandaged hand in patient
supplication. 'My broken abbey', you cried
already crafting your way with words, a claim

shouted from a niche large enough to frame
angelic poses while the Minolta clicked,
a niche in which eight hundred years ago

a monk at vespers planted a flambeau
but did not see me in the shadows. It was
I who found the Holy Grail but,

stealing from the Chapel Perilous, bucked
my toe and tripped. May you be more sure footed
as you pilgrim forth between the weal and woe.

IV

On a visit to our ancestral island you danced
me down to the Blue Lagoon, round as a chalice,
full to the brim with wine distilled to water.

It was that still time when the sea breeze falters
and the mountain wind, asleep in the valley, has not
yet stirred. We stood on the brink, our bright

reflections glowing at the edges in the sapphire light
that glazed the surface to a mirror. I
half expected Excalibur to rise

and amputate my toe but your eyes
were fixed on the fettle of a rebuilt abbey
in which you prayed, a chant of silent bubbles

breaking from your lips. The rowan tree doubled
its image and under its liquid benediction
a china ballerina kissed a china fish.

The doctor breeze, awakened, cooled the bush
rustling a goodbye chorus in the leaves.
The cupped hands holding the chalice quivered

and as the water blurred the abbey crumbled
back to ruin; the rowan, overwatered, returned
its roots to Scotland; the fish wriggled to a line.

The fragile doll spun and splintered, a fine
sawdust, one leg and then an arm, drifting
to the mysterious bottom at the end of time.

TIME AND TIDE

Between the V of the hull
and the XXXs of the verandahed villas
lies the blue sea talking to itself
in ultramarine tautologies of deep debate,
each syllable a wave
foaming into gibberish upon the reef.

To port is Cuba
and the terror of a navigational error;
to starboard
the headlands of Port Antonio like a beached whale
wallowing in shallow water.

Crossing the reef we run aground,
knocking the engine out. In that instant
of stunned silence
the coral claims its right of encrustation,
secreting new monuments for another generation —
the jewelled oval of my wife's astonished mouth,
my son-in-law's bronzed back
bent over the dead wheel,
my daughter's arms, ripening to jade,
locked around her sons,
heads inclined in coined profile,
my right hand, wrist manacled in sand,
groping for the log book and a pen.

FEELING SLIGHTLY ILL-AT-EASE IN SOMEONE ELSE'S HOUSE

These salt eroded seaside villas,
their peeling walls mildewed with gossip,
have tongues as well as ears. Stale
rumours like bad breath seep
through cement, coating the cushions,
fogging the vision
of the glass sliding doors.

Four thin volumes curl together
in the empty built-in bookcase,
crumbling in their covers.
Unsilvered at the edges, a mirror
welcomes its reflection like a friend whose name
it has forgotten and in the powder room
the drivel of a dripping tap
is cocktail conversation down the drain.

The view will compensate, perhaps!
O blemished Sermio, this must be
the season of low tides in the
affairs of men and oceans. No water
shines, only a skeleton
of reef off-shore strewn like the bones
of the Phoenician sailor face down in rocks.

Endurance of a day like this
exhausts the heart. Madam Sosostris,
put your pack of cards
and prophesies away.
Time to retire, to lock the doors
and pull the pale curtains shut.

But the suspicious bed
draws up the linens to its chin
and under thin, soiled sheets
the rust encrusted springs recoil.

CLOCKS

For us the cities of the world build clocks
to count with bell and bong and chime
our stock of hours
stored forever open-eyed
like slashed sacks slowly bleeding time.

All night while others sleep
we trace the mice feet of our thoughts
across the skin of blistered floors,
fingering the scab of our impending deaths,
pretending slumber
rather than couple with adjacent flesh.

We are your proper poets
listening to the beat of fickle hearts,
perplexed alike by truth and false alarms.
All night while clocks unwind
we are concerned why only corpses sleep.

WHAT THE CLOUD SAW

A cloud leans over the edge of the sky,
steals an astonished look at earth
and blanches. Clawed by a rebuking
wind it drifts in pale shreds
to its inexorable death,
the secret of what it might have seen
still sealed behind dissolving lips.

SILENCE

When the accustomed hum which I
have long accepted as the absence
of sound suddenly ceases, the
ensuing silence pours into
my ears like syrup and I become
profoundly deaf.

                I have not heard
oh Lord, the lamentation of
the poor, nor the laughter of
the rich. Nor in my sojourn
in foreign lands has the echo
of the bud unfolding
to a rose disturbed my sleep.

                The summer season
washes across my history
like a sable brush loaded
with water blurring the boundaries
of exact events. I do not
hear their consequences being
watered down.

                By December
the sky cracks and out of its fissures
a cold wind swirls, stripping
the leaves from their branches. They drop
like black tears into the gutters
of cities but I am not awakened
by the splash of their weeping.

                   Age spots
map their dominion on the back of my hands
and a voice whispers through the syrup
'When you are old and your soul is shivering,
the last stitch of its dream unravelling,
pull this poem like a shawl
around your nakedness.' Only
the rags of words are left to warm
the marrow, once more the word made flesh.

KINGSTON/BAGHDAD
(Late Thursday Afternoon, January 15, 1991)

'What a pluperfect afternoon' she cries,
hands to her cheeks. 'Let us take two chairs
into the garden and watch the end of it.'

Yellow ochre air splashes the mountains,
slowly dyeing the city gold, the dome
of Holy Trinity Cathedral glowing like a mosque

in the slanting evening light. On the plain,
cane is burning in the corner of a field,
a finger of smoke beckoning for water.

'Listen' — a finger on her lips. In the distance
a woodpecker's machine-gun burst, the wail
of a car alarm triggered by mistake.

Dragonflies, squadron after squadron,
strafe the terraced lawns, lining up
a bomb run on the city. Ginger lilies

secretly release their scent as a beetle
climbs the bank, inexorable as a tank,
refusing to change its course. Over

the lilac harbour a cloud bellies like a tarp
camouflaging a flank of sky
surrendering its blue. 'I never knew

a bird at rest that does not fold its wings.
What do you make of that?' .... pointing
to a crow perched on the transformer

of a power pole, wings hunched like shoulders
around a thin, red neck — the bird's
unblinking eyes sucking the last light into blackness.

'A lovely evening — but please don't leave me yet'.

ARS LONGA

A.
Pain trickled like etching acid
down Rembrandt's cheek eating
away the cracked impasto and
the lurking umber shadows.
After such a long investment
in the ravages of flesh,
his dying was a white flash
of clear, bare bone.

B.
Pain rooted in Gauguin's balls
shooting like a purple plant
into his brain, emerald leaves
curling tighter and tighter inside
the cavity of his skull. When
there was no more space the suffering
ceased. After such a long
investment in the depravities of flesh,
his dying was a flash
of green garden old as Adam.

C.
Toulouse-Lautrec trying to come
to grips with pain kept clawing
at it above his head as if
he had been amputated and the hurt
incensed the raw, vacated air.
After such a long investment
in the limits of the flesh,
his dying was a final crimson flash
as he crashed into the lintel of a door
carrying his bride across the threshold.

D.
The pain in Hakusai's fingers
allowed him only a second split
between dread and agony
in which to whip the line of brush
around the nude, sequestering
the rising breast,
the lip fluting into smile.
After such a long investment
in the transience of flesh,
his dying was a final flash
of black, a purple afterglow
fading on the paper screen
behind the heavy lidded eyes.

MR. GOODMAN'S LAST VISIT ABROAD

I

Only one of his three daughters had endorsed the trip
but with the cosmic admonition not to fall
for some nubile native girl. Arriving now,
taxi tossed from airport to hotel,
knees locked against the centrifugal
pull of coastal curves,
the trick it seems is not to fall at all.

An unctuous major-domo, gripping his elbow, steers
him to the desk. Eyes still unfocussed
he lifts his misted spectacles and peers
at the white registration card tilted
like a headstone anxious to read its epitaph.

> NAME: David Goodman of New York.
> AGE: Eighty-two.
> OCCUPATION: Retired textile merchant
> RELIGION: One-half Catholic, one half Jew.

With the aplomb of one of his ancestors who
   greeted Crusoe,
the manager confirms he is the only guest,
this being the off-season. The staff though skeletal
is keen, dinner at seven on the patio,
jacket and tie required. But a prodigal
sun unmindful of low housecounts,
coins the light and like a spendthrift gambles
it away. The sea, obsessed, erotic,
squanders wet caresses on the empty beach.

II

After dinner he grips the patio railing,
feet apart, a humped captain on the bridge
of a deserted ocean liner sailing
into the darkness of a night without horizon.
He is surrounded by a sea of empty
tables set for ghosts, the crested napery
fluted into linen shells, the silver
ranked diminuendo to a teaspoon silence.
The deck dips or else the brandy's water-
line is sloshing behind the portholes of his eyes.

Back in his bunk night thoughts hang like bats
inside his brain — like his lisle socks, suspenders
still attached, dangling from the shower
rail. He reaches for the lamp, fingers
jerking back as he recalls the shocking
martyrdom of Merton in Bangkok —
the long silence ending in an astonished scream,
the unused red hot holy words beading
like lava down the flayed flex. The ceiling
fan like a frenetic clock spins off
the minutes of his life, luffing
the curtains and his socks. Here, death filters
through the louvres like the scent of jasmine.

III

His first infidelity. Now that lust
has long since leached away, all that
he remembers is the dressing, her torso leaning
forward in the space between the bed and where
she stood under the nimbus of the skylight;
the quick caress of fingers to each breast
nesting them in lace, the head's flamboyant

toss, the arabesque of swirling hair.
But not the texture of the touching! All numb —
the textile merchant's final curse,
like rubbing nothing between thumb and index
    finger.
He did not tell his wife of the affair
but sweating Catholic guilt, conscience frayed
a little at the edges, he sulked until
one day she asked, 'Is anything the matter?
You look lost'. To which his Jewish id
replied, 'not lost, my dear — perhaps mislaid'.

IV

I found her dead
stretched upon the Persian carpet
in our apartment,
the red skirt,
her outflung hand,
the shattered heart
now part of a new design —
from heaven's height
a small stain.

Her eyes and mouth
were open, her lips
blue as were her fingertips,
cold to my touch.

I shut her eyes
pressing on the lids
but the mouth refused to close,
cheek muscles slack.

Something sacred
had escaped
the passage of her throat
which, gaping, waited
for its return and would not shut.

If I had thread
I would have stitched
the lips together gently
and slowly basted them in a smile
knowing she would not feel the needle.

I rummaged through a drawer —
threadbare — only a dictionary,
Webster's unabridged,
which I reposed upon her breast,
words enough to wish her rest
.....and to prop the jaw.

V

Soon after the funeral he started
talking to himself and writing poetry
which may be the same phenomena
but vice versa. To her he dedicated
his soliloquies and poems, the latter
submitted to the journals once a quarter.
After fourteen years of brusque rejection
slips one of his sonnets was accepted
by a magazine of international
reputation. 'Adam's curse' he muttered,
'One line per year! Son of a bitch, I quit'.

He bound a copy in a red Cordova leather
and laid it gently by the Webster,
still bravely unabridged but badly battered.

VI

Dawn is breakfast served on a silver platter
headed from the sea to his verandah
by a black aphrodite who he either
conjured in a dream or being real,
one arm akimbo like the handle
of the terracotta vase upon the table,
coughs discreetly and vanishes into the corona
of the sun, leaving a dishevelled Adam
to the seduction of another day.

> In late afternoon
> he staggers from his room
> to the water's edge,
> at his back the spotlight of the sun
> shining through the selvedge of his skin.
>
> A sign commands:
> 'No topless tanning'
> but not a naked sole
> much less a naked body
> imprints the beach which curls,
> freshly raked,
> around the deserted bay.
>
> He is uneasy with the waste.
> All this for one old man?
> It is indecent beyond words —
> some offering to the gods

is due. Knees trembling
he drops his ancient trunks,
tries to straighten the carved
curvature of his spine
and on matchstick legs,
humming in time
to Colonel Bogey's march
shuffles naked down the beach,
parading past the reviewing stand
of the hotel.

At the other end, his left hand,
pellucid and blue veined,
visors his watering eyes
sighting back along the line of footprints,
along the row of one legged roundels,
the empty beach chairs sinking
into their shadows,
his discarded trunks
like a pink almond leaf
catching the light where he had stood.

Right hand on his cock
he commands the waves to come.
And one swell,
heaving with an extra passion
swirls up the littoral,
sucks up the sand around the fallen
loin cloth and drags it out to sea.

A cone of clouds accumulates
on the horizon like a volcano
but battered by his laughter blows away
and his undulating trunks, heavy
with salt, saturated with the secrets
of David Goodman's crotch
sink slowly in the undertow.

THE OTHER ISLAND

The cable calling him to active
duty in Japan trembled
in his mother's hand. She had cried,
'I will never see you again'
and took to bed but asthma had taught her
how to sleep with eyes half open,
pupils pulled up under the lids,
mouth half open too, still echoing
its oracle. In World War I,
two days before the armistice,
a German gunner had stitched a row
of medals into her brother's chest,
their red ribbons trickling down.
For the hard journey back to Jamaica
The army packed his binoculars
in a tiny coffin lined with silk.
She would not let him play with it.

II

Into the door of his Air Force room
was hinged a smaller door, a flap
through which Yasuko, his maid,
would peek, down on her knees, careful
not to ruffle his imperial sleep,
still curious about the colour
of this conqueror's skin. She always spied
when he was standing naked in the middle
of the room. Their eyes would meet and she would giggle,
holding the sleeve of the kimono
over her mouth — the same gesture his mother
used to cover her protruding teeth.
Yasuko perfumed his exile
bringing her consolations with tiny steps

to his off-duty hours, alleging
her love in English less tenuous
than his limping Japanese.
Their body language tested every
consonant and vowel, slurring
only when they talked of islands.
Like her neighbour, he explained,
old women in Jamaica swept
the yard with tied-together branches,
green brooms that sprouted if you
planted them. Fujiyama
was like Mount Fancy looking from the gap
toward Buff Bay, its slopes as lovely
and symmetrical.   Jealous islands!
She touched his cheek and whispered, 'I think
that you are not completely black'.

III

A southern colonel, veteran
of countless bamboo battles, drawled:
'Never tell them you're returning Stateside.
Marriage is their one way ticket
to paradise. When you explain
that miscegenation is illegal
they take the law into their own hands,
so to speak, cut off your prick
with one of their Samurai razors,
so quick you hardly feel the swipe.
But there you are sitting upright
on the tatami, legs spread,
blood pulsing from an interior pipe —
and where do you tie the tourniquet, boy,
around your waist?'

IV

Below him in the auditorium
black heads bowed like crotchets to each other
along the stave of seats, composing a hum
of conversation. Such homogeneous
genes — not a distracting blond minim
in the house. Fed up with the twang
of samisens and geisha girls with flour
dusted faces wailing dissonances
into his untutored Caribbean ear,
he had booked a ticket for a post-war
classical recital, expecting
an empty house. Gieseking,
who had played for Hitler, warming
his fingers now for Debussy.
There were no empty seats and at the door,
instead of programmes ushers sold
folio editions of the score.
At the bottom of each page
the white sheets fluttered, changing direction
like birds flying in formation.
Then it was over and between the echoing
whispers of the music and the passion
of the applause, the samisens were silenced
as were the calypsos in his blood.
He could no longer hear the klaxons at Pearl Harbour
or at Iwo Jima the feral thud
of shells. It was civilised to press the master
for an encore — that ancient cry
he shouted louder than the rest,
waving his Air Force cap, 'Banzai! Banzai!'

V

Bang on the door. 'Telephone call
for you lieutenant'. He ran down
the hall in jockey shorts to where
the receiver dangled. 'I was sorry
to hear about your mother's passing.
I just got the news....' Crackle. Crackle.
The line went dead. A cable had been sent
but war had intercepted it.
Among so many deaths what was notable
about this one? A severe attack of asthma,
an accidental overdose of morphine?

VI

He stood at sunset on the brink
of bomb bruised Tokyo
watching a solitary fishing boat
cut from the river into the bay,
the fisherman standing in the stern
rolling a single oar from side
to side. Back home it would have been
a cotton tree canoe, rowed blindly backward,
towing an island. This squint eyed
craft, hull high, looked where it was going,
not where it had been, the blade
of the oar unscrolling in Japanese
the warning of a wake he could not decipher.

A wave of homesickness slopped into nausea.

About the author

Ralph Thompson's family on his mother's side goes back three generations in Jamaica, a mixture of crypto-Jewish and Irish stock. It was staunchly Catholic and 'claimed to be white'. His mother's marriage lasted only three years and he was brought up in a household of 'intellectually brilliant but poor and highly eccentric aunts and uncles'.

His education was heavily influenced by the Jesuits through high school in Jamaica and university in America. After completing a Doctor of Law degree at Fordham University, New York, he served for two years as an officer in the US Air Force in Japan, after which he returned to Jamaica and started his career as businessman, painter and poet. The father of four children, he lives with his wife in Kingston.

Ralph Thompson has given public service under both political administrations in Jamaica and was awarded the Commander of Distinction in the Jamaican National Honours of 1988.

Throughout his business career, first painting and then poetry have been the ordering passions in his life.